THE PORTAGE POETRY SERIES

SERIES TITLES

Users with Access: New and Selected Poems
Brandon Krieg

Flu Season
Katie Kalisz

No Trouble Staying Awake
Teresa Scollon

Another Native Tongue
Susan Riley Clarke

Catch & Release
Lauren Crawford

Steelhead
Lauren K. Carlson

The Coronation of the Ghost
Benjamin Gantcher

The Stone Tries to Understand the Hands
Susannah Sheffer

Red Camaro
Dwaine Rieves

Where Babies Come From
Ori Fienberg

Cuttings
Hannah Dow

Forgive the Animal
Sarah Pape

Love as Invasive Species
Ellen Kombiyil

They Were Horrible Cooks
Allison Whittenberg

The New Life
Wendy Wisner

Restoring Prairie
Margaret Rozga

Table with Burning Candle
Julia Paul

A Bright Wound
Sarah A. Etlinger

The Velvet Book
Rae Gouirand

Listening to Mars
Sally Ashton

Glitter City
Bonnie Jill Emanuel

The Trouble with Being a Childless Only Child
Michelle Meyer

Happy Everything
Caitlin Cowan

Dear Lo
Brady Bove

Sadness of the Apex Predator
Dion O'Reilly

Do Not Feed the Animal
Hikari Miya

The Watching Sky
Judy Brackett Crowe

Let It Be Told in a Single Breath
Russell Thorburn

The Blue Divide
Linda Nemec Foster

Lake, River, Mountain
Mark B. Hamilton

Talking Diamonds
Linda Nemec Foster

Poetic People Power
Tara Bracco (ed.)

The Green Vault Heist
David Salner

There is a Corner of Someplace Else
Camden Michael Jones

Everything Waits
Jonathan Graham

We Are Reckless
Christy Prahl

Always a Body
Molly Fuller

Bowed As If Laden With Snow
Megan Wildhood

Silent Letter
Gail Hanlon

New Wilderness
Jenifer DeBellis

Fulgurite
Catherine Kyle

The Body Is Burden and Delight
Sharon White

Bone Country
Linda Nemec Foster

Not Just the Fire
R.B. Simon

Monarch
Heather Bourbeau

The Walk to Cefalù
Lynne Viti

The Found Object Imagines a Life: New and Selected Poems
Mary Catherine Harper

Naming the Ghost
Emily Hockaday

Mourning
Dokubo Melford Goodhead

Messengers of the Gods: New and Selected Poems
Kathryn Gahl

After the 8-Ball
Colleen Alles

Careful Cartography
Devon Bohm

Broken On the Wheel
Barbara Costas-Biggs

Sparks and Disperses
Cathleen Cohen

Holding My Selves Together: New and Selected Poems
Margaret Rozga

Lost and Found Departments
Heather Dubrow

Marginal Notes
Alfonso Brezmes

The Almost-Children
Cassondra Windwalker

Meditations of a Beast
Kristine Ong Muslim

The Worse For Wear

Steeped in early-aughts pop-culture, experimental poetics, and the absurdities of collegiate and political bureaucracy, *The Worse For Wear* is a guide for how to just get through the day in America, and then how to collect those days into a meaningful life. From early, awkward teenage crushes, to the disillusionments of middle age, this book is for those of us trying to map out how we got from there to here, to forgive our younger selves, and to accept our current ones. Hard-earned truths are both unfrocked in blunt, direct confrontation, and costumed-up in rich, joyous language. Super-smart, super-funny, super-gay, and super-heart-wrenching, Goldsmith's work is a celebration of poetry as one of our flawed humanity's greatest, redeeming habits.

—ROBIN LAMER RAHIJA
author of *Inside Out Egg*

How does it feel to be in your body? asks Jenna Goldsmith in her fresh, important new collection, *The Worse For Wear*, in which juxtapositions abound. *What you mean is/the skin holds in so much/ What I'm thinking about/ is what the skin holds out* . . . But it is not only the body that Goldsmith is thinking about: almost everything becomes fodder for interrogation, for resistance, for experience. What spills out, what cannot be contained finds its way to forms that both resist and shore up their subject. Experimentation meets everyday life in these poems that teem with virtuosic intensity. This collection offers something I don't often find: surprise.

—SARAH A. ETLINGER
author of *A Bright Wound*

The Worse For Wear

poems

Jenna Goldsmith

CORNERSTONE PRESS
UNIVERSITY OF WISCONSIN-STEVENS POINT

Cornerstone Press, Stevens Point, Wisconsin 54481
Copyright © 2026 Jenna Goldsmith
www.uwsp.edu/cornerstone

Printed in the United States of America.

Library of Congress Control Number: 2026931108
ISBN: 978-1-968148-31-7

Cornerstone Press titles are produced in courses and internships offered by the Department of English at the University of Wisconsin–Stevens Point.

DIRECTOR & PUBLISHER
Dr. Ross K. Tangedal

EXECUTIVE EDITORS
Jeff Snowbarger, Freesia McKee

EDITORIAL DIRECTOR
Brett Hill

SENIOR EDITORS
Paige Biever, Reilly Crous

PRESS STAFF
Allison Lange, Sophie McPherson, Sam Bjork, Madison Schultz, Autumn Vine

ALSO BY JENNA GOLDSMITH:

I own every bell that tolls me.

—Neko Case

Great Expectations

Wedged between the Mayor's shaking
hand and succulent party favors
we are the other's mirror

in houndstooth tops,
in edging bodies

down the hall
in rubber shoes,
in the way

you tell me I have a face.

What you mean is
the skin holds in so much.

What I'm thinking about
is what the skin holds out.

My thirty-year superstition
blows flimsy in the afternoon's
gale.

To be clean
I'd have to give up great-

great grandma's edict:
never use soap on your face.
You know? That's a lot.

Never mind she meant
bar soap and I misunderstood.

That's a lot
of ignoring to now just   see.

It's hard to give up
what you've never done.

After the first wash
I shine red and hide
this new forehead feeling in hair.

Is this clean? What have I
done?

What else can
I let blow through the storefront door?

What else will I give up—
        mask borne of
        kin I've never met

        —for your
        eyebrows?

Valentine's Day

for KJ

When my legs swing
    out from under me

I don't know your plans.
    You simply kneel

down, knees pressed
    against a sandy-slick

gym floor to catch my
    hot cheek.

From some periphery
    your crouch

says   *you're fine*
    and I know I am

even as blood
    closes over my temple,

edges the hairline
    like the semi-circle

of mouths circling
    my pitched frame.

It might be a lie—
    the circle of mouths—

never peeked to look,
    knew better than that.

I do know my own lips parted
        not in a circle

but in a straight line
        for some sound.

Were you there? (*dontanswerthat*)

Nobody knows anything in high school
        or anyone.
Now tell my everything.

You can start by explaining
        the white shorts,
        your free throws,

where you sat in Spanish class,
        the white ribbon in your hair.

I thought I knew your destiny,
        certainly better than I knew my own.

What I thought
        was new
        was me.

I didn't have to worry about you
        the way I did others
        and myself.

When my face heals, a little
        voice imagines thanking you.
        I give you a chocolate from Valentine's Day,
        an excuse to gift a memory,
        something sweet and impermanent
        to disappear inside you.

To forget, if you—
     to my relief—
    choose.

To remember, if you—
     to my relief—
    choose.

At the Water Tower

You're getting married
and I'm thinking
of the water tower,
tip of Broad Street,
grass sheaths stuck
under terry cloth, spun
open and draped
sidelong over
thighs. I'm messed
up on the details.

Was there
a pool in Annette's backyard?
Were you wet
headed? For sure backs
sloped the gentle grade
to the water tower,
or was the ground
flat but for
divots boned
by skidding kneecaps,
zippered creases open
to hold curved
theres and
         theres?
Necks bent up
to the tower's
enormous bulb.

It was—*must have
been*—night: muggy,
your friends outlined

shapes standing aghast over
us and this wasn't even the last time.
I wish I remembered
the jeans I wore, if my
hair yet cut
short, clean
or dirty. Had I given
it up, was it the you and I
before or after
the movie theater?

All scenes your
abominable memory
reasonably released,
but I know you remember
the tower.

I saw it.

On some level,
on some plane of
a near reality,
we're at the water tower,
bodies arched bridges
but to ourselves
who are still us
who are still us

Intimacy

After we meet it's soap for lotion

Lotion for toothpaste

Toothpaste for eye cream

Eye cream for lip balm

Lip balm for perfume

Perfume for mouthwash

Mouthwash for laundry detergent

Laundry detergent for underwear

Underwear for tea towel

Tea towel for t-shirt

T-shirt for tank top

Tank top for sock

Sock for other sock

Other sock for handkerchief

Handkerchief for hand towel

Hand towel for paper towel

Paper towel for water bottle

Water bottle for dish soap

Dish soap for hand soap

Hand soap for half and half

Half and half for sour cream

Sour cream for cream cheese

Cream cheese for crème fraiche

Crème fraiche for yogurt

Yogurt for butter

Butter for bread

Bread for biscuits

Biscuits for black tea

Black tea for blackberries

Blackberries for raisins

Raisins for chocolate

Chocolate for gravy

Gravy for marmalade

Marmalade for music

Music for lightbulb

Lightbulb for watering can

Watering can for bicycle

Bicycle for blue jeans

Blue jeans for bare skin

Bare skin for bed

Bed for alarm clock

Alarm clock for sleep

Sleep for soap

Soap for lotion

Confessions Part II

When you are a young person
and living everyday
you don't know you are
making your own life's history.

My history is now
in the books.
I remember it in the one way
it happened.

Does that change the way I act today?
Like putting on my shoes
or the music I listen to:
Yes.
Now I know how to do everything.

I'm a much different person than
I was in 2004 but I avoid that.
I still wear UGG boots and Curious by Britney Spears,
still keep stacks of discs in my glove box.

My brain is sharpest when turned
to 2004, so I'm offended when my girlfriend
tells me I'm too old for 2004.

I like most 2004 bodies,
bumping 2004 tracks,
and eating 2004 food.

My dad's emotional dependence on
the 1970s comes into
sharp relief now.
I'd apologize if I could for making fun of you.
2004 teaches forgiveness.

Upon Reading Lytle Shaw's Obituary of Lyn Hejinian

Obituaries by poets
for other poets
is how it's done
do other vocations
do this
like postal
workers

> *in lieu of*
> *flowers send*
> *mail*

post mortem
I read the
obituary because of
who it is
for   who it is
by
chicken or egg
it was like
reading their latest
publication
post
mortem

something weird
I thought was
she'll never have
another
book
not poor
Larry Ochs

Poor children
her poems are
over

then as news
spreads
certain kinds of
poets will post
on Facebook
another weird
thought is
my dissertation
isn't contemporary
full of
mostly dead
poets
someday all
three will be gone
whoa
I am rent
in two

I learn a lot
about her
from Lytle Shaw's
obit in *Jacket2*
Lyn's first name
a shortening
last name an ex
husband's
younger than I
thought older
than I thought
just
human things

what I have of her
several poetry books
glimpse of her
at the hotel
bar in Oakland
names almost
touching
on the conference
program
two anthologies loose
on the car floor
a whole ass
dissertation

next year's writing
conference will be
a lot of
Hejinian
panels

sad sad sad sad sad
I'm
stalling the ending
I can't
push out
can't get
quite right

Threshold

the portal only goes one way and I'm still
thinking about this   how doors and
windows   work   don't work
          how this is   the threshold
the terrarium traps the lightening bug
cop's spike strip ends the chase in my
computer game

you and   then my mind
morning and mourning   *oh this*
again   birth:

the baby decides to turn around mid-
slide   first taste of stale   air too
much   *this isn't for me*   who
would choose what they cannot see

air and gravity

over the pillowed pink of an inside
forever   what do we call this one foot
in front of the other world   revolving
door   trap door   mouth   I
think of your one world and your oth-
er world and your other world and

I lose

count

On the Day We Meet I Express Gratitude

Pens nametags SPF   Be on my podcast
oh I work for Janssen oh I'm not
a nurse haha Special K   did you see
the Fire Chief   did you see that
chair that end table   tall in the back   let's get one
of the Mayor shaking hands ok get   a little closer
wait I'll leave with
you squeeze in   you yes you   I'm
thanking you   in the eggshell corner
we're on something
about art something about high school
something about art

Ekphrasis

God everywhere   but
there is no outer space
this is where I contradict myself
overnight   the plant greens
gray   black   pink   first sun at dawn   hits: plasma
first   sip of cold water   on a July afternoon
you teach me how   to   let them   let them

touch me   on the street
when I tell you   when I'm telling on myself
what is your name?   when I'm teaching it to others

In Spring I get bangs   wash my face
should've known something   moved
old jeans   fit new
gold shoes   Spring again   Summer
old poems in boxes
love notes: plasma
                                                       mustard couch
for petty tiffs to land: plasma

Looking on   :plasma
not of bones but the   combination kind
                                             sun   moon   kind
New moon for people   full moon to kiss necks

Jean Meeus Comes to Us as a Raccoon in a Garbage Can

After the new moon in May
        I run out of calories
        sit on a curb
        because I
        can't stand
        but you don't know that

Our bodies break in the theatre seats
        we vow to snag the fold ups
        next time and I beg the moon
        silently and so desperately
        there will be a next time
                but you don't know that

In the parking lot at the school it's only just
        summer and the rest stretches
        out before us like a dark alley but you
        help me see the days as one and one
        and the traffic light that's
        been stuck on yellow reverses to green
                but you don't know that

Just before the parking lot and the curb and the
        green light Jean Meeus comes to us as a
        raccoon in a garbage can
        dark eyes
        telling me what mammals you'll permit
        and I'll stow this away like the
        mice in your basement dining on
        dark chocolate
        but you don't know that

The new moon is the only phase we cannot see
    you are entirely
    in your body
    I make sure I'm still
    breathing and I'll admit something I want,
    lunation: yours
    but you don't know that

In May I coast on your tailwinds
        in June I ask the new moon
        for help again. This is only
        my third time doing this.
    I turn forward
    my red hat's brim, lay flat on a
    wood slab near a shrub and a spider web.
    I ask what am I doing what am I
    doing what am I doing who will
    love me who will love me who will—
    but you don't know that.

Nobody knows that one.

Relief v.1: An Erasure of Entanglement

*from a period of emails starting April 4, 2022, and
ending April 5, 2023*

We're so happy
read her

O

                                  stay

Relief

                relief

                          Do you want me   is there time

                  for me to   be present

       you

                 looking to   you

   I am   her poem

   Glad   my interest to
   Reach   she   thrilled   this is working

                     on my Poet

we want to

                  I'm needing   her

       this is working out to be

Relief

      relief

    Our Poet   poet
                  She is   a
   good   good

   O

Relief

      relief

     you get it. We are
           We have
           one of your artists

with a   poem

Please let me   this is possible
             I know
             you

Relief

      relief

Notice
This email and its attachments
if you are   if you have
please

if you

go

Say Gold

On the topic of missing
I don't missingyou don't
longing   you ask is this it
what you grasp for   let's call it
                          let's call it   a positive resonance
and on the topic of   longing   is longing
it's for simple parts
curves of wrist   tell me
                    my   ha   nds
what you can make out   follicle
                                            fingerprints
and on the topic of the room   from across the room
tell me what you see
I see bars everywhere
gold   close your eyes   poppies in the hallway
                                      red   yellow   orange
and on the topic of faces   wash my face
say mine
gold it
how many girls have told you   after   say gold
in their notebooks   your name means what
in their minds   written it
                                        initialed your poems

What Story Can We Tell Better

gold tutu / trapped behind / the couch / in your studio / and so in / that way still / with us / or that / it's lost / forever / cinched 'round a / stranger's waist / asleep beneath the / Midway / marquee / (damn those murals!) / or tumbleweeding / down 2nd Street / or stuck in the / bushes / where we / danced / held / hands to / balance on the / sidewalk / where you / shucked off / your gold / to keep us / safe / and we / knew why / It could have / gone either way / But that night / you / were my / golden rabbit / of the / masquerade / still your favorite / night for / that picture / for Joan and / Tina / still mine / for the first / time I watched / you dance / smoke / first time you / touched my / hand / stomach / first scent / of your / hair so close / to my face / what you tell me / first / what you show me / first / poppies in the hallway / first deep / breaths behind / the steering wheel / on Market Street / on State Street / on Jefferson Street / on Church Street / They / were firsts / they were firsts / they were firsts

Senescence

sunk in this sea floor's relief   [hi]   [I like your hair]
[pretty shirt]   holding his fourth arm   [thanks]
detached from his body   [who is he?]   pointing [his] [you
know] [him]   pointing [without it all he'll do is age]
[die in days]   [not like us] [free] [your arms so
soft]   [I'll never die]   her arms   [let me hold you]
arms   [I like to hold you]   oh her arms
[let's bury him after the storm] oh
[let's live forever]

Relief v.2: An Erasure in Pronouns

from a period of emails starting April 4, 2023
and ending April 5, 2023

We're   you   us   We   her

you'd   you
you'd

you   you   me

me

all   you

I   her

I I   you   My
our she   I

Someone our   you
your

me
she
our   we've
I'm
I'm   her

I'm   our
I

their
your

me   you   —she
your

        you   We

                        you   you

        I   you   We

        We're   we   your

                              you   your

                        me   you   I

            you   you

Body Awareness

How does it feel to be in your body[1]?

---

[1] We communicate in voices we don't have
share ghost stories over
sycamored hills before
the emerald of late spring
switches to smoke,
car's turn signal
a metronome of our hearts.

Hard to believe
I nearly missed this
Illinois just-summer
with you.

Downtown we eat
and watch
rainbowed strangers
wonder who
can tell just by
looking how
your body pains,
my world spins.

But then, the knife
of joy, a memory of what is true,
the questions colors ask
pink   green   white
the blue of it all
that fold is a noun
          and a verb
and so is kiss
and so is hurt
and maybe so is
          body.

I Never Mean It When I Say I'm Sorry

for the desire   a poet's desire
        too much, too quiet,
        too adding, too adding,
        too subtracting, too
        protracting, too attaching.

Sorry for the singing   for the warm water
        for what   for what
        I don't know,
        no idea. For flying
        in the dark, arms outstretched
        like zombies or my kid
        self in a power outage
        mom where's the candle   where's
        the flashlight.

For let me help you,
for let me don't help you,
for the easter egg,
        that one I'm not sorry for but

I'm sorry.   So sorry.
For the try less
for the try more
for the harder
for the lesser and the
        lesser I have   the
        more I give and
        I've always been
        sorry

about time

that there is never enough
too much

for these things
for those things

for that thing I
    did at that place
    with the people
    and the money
we do what we
    can what we
    can do what
    I can do.

Proprioception

Knees no feet   walk me down the street
Breathes for me walks   for me   sinks me
sings me   into the ground   rainwater.
Not just that: standing kicking moving
side to side   kicking   jumping lunging standing
kicking   kicking.

Yawn no jaw   I've forgotten how to speak
jaws don't hold me   up   walk me down the street
whisper   hold my tongue loose
I have teeth   roof of mouth.

Shoulders no spine   always on my mind
what I should remember   bottoms of feet
backs of knees   lifting legs up stairs
opens the door   washes my face.

I remember
I remember

Don't you   maybe jaw

You shouldn't   jaw won't

Maybe   back lowers

back down

You

Goodnight

At the Museum

Small fish and
      snakes are a no for you

each mammal has
      made me sad

at the taxidermied fawn it clicks
      lock eyes

           the animals weren't

caught and stuffed by museum staff
      stolen young or old

for us three and our
      afternoon at the museum

so at the stiff badger
      lion and fox

I'm released
      unburdened now

settle beside the fawn
      a matching game

for us three
      now on the museum's lawn
      sigh and wave goodbye

we played at something
      but what

Relief v.3: An Erasure in Reckonings

from a period of emails starting April 4, 2023,
and ending April 5, 2023

We're so happy   We're starting

                                   you can stay

                                   you want me there

                              I am waiting

I am glad   I am thrilled

                                   I'm finalizing
          I'm needing

     I'm not sure

     Please let me

                         She is

     You'll have

          We hope

I left you   hopefully   We are

                                              We have

          We're doing
               we could

                              Please let me

                                   now

With Sorrow

Words I already know when I read *Dobbs* for the first time:
    stare decisis   *amici* viability Tay-
    Sachs   *Ante*   *Casey*   *Griswold*
    precedent law   regime   interference
    rights   *Obergefell*   *Loving* 14 *supra*
    Lawrence   fetal sterilized   just-
    ice *Barnette*   dissent

Words I must look up when I read *Dobbs* for the first time:
    women liberty   life light death yes-
    terday wonder   nightmare   futurestate
    womb but   people   me-
    n intimate Justice medical self   no

Weller

after Gertrude Stein

Hope you're weller   weller   soon
getting weller   soon

you're getting weller   now weller
now weller
help me get weller

                                        now we're   weller
I'm weller
You're weller

                                                oh   we
ller

                                        ohhhhh   we
Relief   inside

                                violet   bright white
So weller now
So much weller   when we're   weller
we

                                                wash my face
And we   were
And they   were   weller
And we   were   weller
And they   were   so   weller
                                                so   weller

And oh   we   were
And oh   we   were

                                                        so weller
When you came over   so weller
        weller
                        I was   more
When I came
                much   more
                weller.   over you were so

35

Well   well   well.
I said   it: weller

Did you   say it   weller?
I did   say it   weller?

Weller   say it   now   yes
I'll say it first: weller
You'll say it next: weller

                                                                        You
like it.   You
like it.   You
like it.   You
l—

there's always a *(repeated many times throughout, forming a heart shape)*

there's always a villain

Vestibular Weakness

It always starts this way: pull left shoulder away from left
ear   depress cranium cradle neck spine skull and neck
again   myofascial's a new word to me   muscles in the scalp
I've arrived

on this woman's table   can't walk a straight line   she
doesn't know I'm a poet, only that I write poems   I spin
a wheel with my feet   we watch videos of her golf prodigy
middle schooler on the

NBC Sports YouTube channel   never respected golf until
today   he's a smart boy she says   I say don't send him to
any university in our town and she nods solemnly   I regret
that   I'm just

mad at my shoulders   slouched so long I've shortened those
muscles and compressed my right rib so it sits inside its
neighbor rib like two crammed siblings in a van's backseat
on a

family vacation   I've feared becoming my hump-backed
Great Aunt Peg and well here I am   things shift within me
the space between my shoulder and elbow isn't as it once was

please allow this upsetness worthy of my age.

Self-observer

after Eileen Myles

Happy husband
grow your
wallflower
marriage
grow
your two kids
in a pot
you couldn't be
a wallflower
if you
tried
I on the
other hand cried
wouldn't
leave the house
without poems
I wasn't like
that before
then
wallflower
you say
wasn't
like that
before then
I say wasn't
like that before
wallflower
did you know where
wallflowers
grow
Chicago

just kidding
I mean the word
wallflower
Philadelphia
just kidding again
I really know nothing
about cities

Happy husband
grow your sex-
      less marriage in
a pot
face me
west on your
wall   wall-
   flower
display me
leering
from the
corner
where I've been
hung

Basket's Lament

I, basket
basket telephone
pole basket
poem, poem basket
lay, basket lay.

Pétanque, basket
rock basket, wheel
wagon, basket
get in the wagon
basket   wagon
  basket   wagon
and
don't give him coffee and
there are rules for dogs.

Hemingway, basket
basketway, heming
heming, basketway.

Rest rest rest
rest   rest.

Coat basket clean,
sheep basket shear,
there are rules for dogs
rules basket   roll.

Early 2004 is still 2003

because of how years work.
The five of us remember it
better than yesterday
because of how memories work.

Nowadays we want to get off
the earth's surface,
escape high winds and pandemics,
unhinged oranges and his adherents.

In 2003 on its way to 2004,
us five were interested in
more earthly delights,
Janet's nipple and Shandi's
hot tub sex.

The world was not so bad
so much as a springboard
to the moon,
2004 like the
high beams of Sara's Corsica,
shuttle-cutting night,
and later night.

A colleague dies

of
sudden infection.

I am sad
and she was nice.
I don't know
what that means.

The emails between us, and
the very young daughters.

She studied sentences and
punctuation;
who loves language that much?

I whisper
to my girlfriend
I love you
        but just in my mind

      over and over

The Way That We Live

I watch a lot of *The L Word* that year
which has almost nothing to do with space
except that in the new millennium
my eyes are made of little stars
and inside my belly are 1s and 0s:
for Shane and
her little spiky rattail, rosary
I pray to, pretend to touch
in my pocket
though I don't think girls like her
exist.

I won't call Carmen extra-terrestrial
though I've a better chance
of being scooped and prodded
in a ship far above my bedroom in
Illinois than lap danced
to a BETTY remix
in Studio City.

Burn tout

What's the status of work orders for lightbulbs in my office?

Let's Contribute to a Community Free of Sexual Misconduct

After an Email from *** President on 18 Nov 2020

Just a gentle reminder that we each of us have a personal and
  shared responsibility to contribute to a community
  free of sexual misconduct and harassment

a gentle reminder that almost all employees are considered
  "responsible employees" and must report any alle-
  gation of sexual misconduct or discrimination or
  harassment, but some employees are not considered
  "responsible employees" and thus have no respon-
  sibility to do the right thing and in fact won't and
  likely don't and indeed didn't

a gentle reminder that this is not a reminder. This is a re-
  quest and also not a request so much as a demand.
  "Responsible employee" has certain rules, and those
  rules can be found at this link, and if you are not a
  "responsible employee," please don't click on this
  link. Instead, simply refer to nothing. ***'s values are
  not your values and you are a valued member of our
  community

a gentle reminder that I am the *** President and have three
  daughters. This means I am writing in subtext, and
  the subtext is that if you harass my daughters, I will
  fuck you up. My daughters go to a different uni-
  versity. With that said, I am committed to policies
  that seek to end sexual misconduct and harassment
  against daughters and will, if you trust me, person-
  ally redirect your report to the Equal Opportunity
  Office

a gentle reminder not to investigate an alleged incident
            yourself, particularly if you are the victim of the inci-
            dent and possess every detail. We have an office that
            does that for you, and several that don't. You will
            never be asked for evidence, for we have no use for
            it. You will be the alleged with no proof. If we built
            a metaphor with a house at the bottom of a hillside
            and a mudslide after a storm, where she is the mud-
            slide and you are the house and the mudslide is full
            of rock and tree parts and mud, and you, the home
            at the bottom of the failing hillside, are unequivo-
            cally destroyed. But the destruction is really only on
            your side because thankfully this university believes
            in restorative justice. The mudslide will get help, and
            each of its parts—rock, tree, mud—ever so gently
            lifted back to their exact, rightful, precarious, places
            before the storm that caused their deterioration and
            eventual destruction of the home, that is, you

a gentle reminder that I care about Title IX, the rolling back
            of Title IX regulations, the rolling front of Title
            IX regulations, the ebb and flow, the rolling side
            to side, the roiling sea of fair and full investigation,
            the raining down of impartiality, the weather of it
            all, sometimes a storm, sometimes a drought, the
            precipitous precipitation of due process reports
            and sexual misconduct to support harassment and
            federal state law and accused plaintiffs, paper tigers,
            research. Wednesday November 18 2020 17:01:58
            Pacific Standard Time the President's office, dear,
            dearest community member

Join me. Be so gentle with me. Your commitment, dear
            community member, is essential and very appre-
            ciated dot com. Please call this number if you are

sexually harassed. Please call this number if you are sexual harassment. I encourage all of those who have been sexually harassed to speak to someone and I encourage all of those who are sexual harassment to speak to someone. Your commitment, too, is essential to this effort and very much appreciated.

Runaway Jury

Will
Dean from Engineering
believe me—

Administrator who
owned a
hardware store
or was it a drapery shop?

Colleague
a former chef
turned professor
turned rancher
of horses and grapes.

Quasi-Provost
once an Executive
at Nordstrom, here now
and there then
power of the purse.

The one who failed organic chemistry
as an undergraduate
painter, now computer scientist,
newspaper writer in Alaska,
veteran who comes from where I do,
veteran who paints,
veteran who we suspect wears
molar necklaces
stolen off bodies buried in his backyard.

Painters are more common than you think.

All the way up the line
and side to side,
jury of my peers,
responsible for nothing
really
but they could be
and would I make it
in that case?

Heart Gut

In poetry group
I try to explain how

        aspiration
        inspiration   travel
        inclination   listening
        funding   working   closing
        the eyes   beginning again
        pulling the drawstring tight
        unfurling one's own flag to surrender
        writing one's own story to quell the bother
        rubbing the sharp edge of one's longing to
        round the fall
        crescendoing a song
        singing the giving up
        letting the feeling
        of feeling

in the circle of poets
that's what the poem teaches us
that technically the heart can be left out

that technically the heart
of the

        aspiration
        inspiration   travel
        inclination   listening
        funding   working   closing
        the eyes   beginning again
        pulling the drawstring tight
        unfurling one's own flag to surrender

writing one's own story to quell the bother
rubbing the sharp edge of one's longing to round the
fall
crescendoing a song
singing the giving up
letting the feeling
of feeling

is heart gut

finding the one end of the string and
finding the other end of the string and bringing
the ends together to tie into a knot

recovering a memory
of reading Virginia Woolf
writing on an empty stomach and
how this translates into the ways
in which we keep ourselves empty
so that we may be women

ruminating on love

always writing the longest poem
everyday waking up to the longest day

the opposite of heart gut
is heart outside of gut, is

      aspiration
      inspiration   travel
      inclination   listening
      funding   working   closing
      the eyes   beginning again
      pulling the drawstring tight

unfurling one's own white flag to surrender
writing one's own life story to quell the bother
rubbing the sharp edge of one's longing to round the
fall
crescendoing a song
singing the giving up
letting the feeling
of feeling

heart gut

can any place be home?

if I put sagebrush in my mouth
will I become here
sit me in a covered wagon
isolate me in the tall trees

Bunny Food

The cat,
not my cat,
needs nourished.

Her food is wet, the
wet you cannot
imagine evaporating

ever. In the
desert, the wet
mirage worth running to
because of the
promise of drink.

But to keep her
alive, the sopping food
isn't enough.

It needs pills and potions,
powder of something
I don't understand
from a pill I cut myself.

Two squeezes
of lysine
balance in
droplets on the mountain's
top.

Whatever is the squeezes
makes them unabsorbable
to whatever is not the squeezes.

Three elements—
        mirage, powder, droplets—
distinct: brown,
darker brown, white.

.

Suppose the Room Just Got Brighter

Suppose the cherries on the neighbor's property were for us
       when we snuck out in the
       dark we weren't stealing
Suppose the door wasn't rotting from the bottom up
Suppose the wind
Suppose the green hose a snake
Suppose every garden box a garden
Suppose the room just got brighter
Suppose the vultures flying above the mud flats
       had an eye on our hair

Suppose the ocean was seamless rivers
Suppose the rules weren't so rigid
       no consequences when I didn't follow them
Suppose there were no consequences
Suppose we ate supper and everything was your favorite
Suppose supper
Suppose the direction you were running was west
       And I knew because you ran into the sea
Suppose I sat at the window awed and waited

Suppose I saw you coming back, wet as anything—sopping
       still floating
       very wet—simply walking up the street
Suppose I had waited there struck, watching

Suppose the room just got brighter

       I sat in my high tower above the sea and every wave a
       whale, every rock a seal's face, every clam and
       crab in communion, caverns in the bay, buzzards
       in and out, wind, toil, food, the sea, the tide, taffy on
       the table, suppose the cherries under a midnight moon
       were ours, suppose the moon, suppose the cherries

Leftovers

Young and gay
I believe I will be alone forever.

This goes without question.
I am unemotional about the fact
and the fates are clear.

So in eight grade
I realize I can love girls through
a metabolic process,
almost digest a piece of them
so they become part of me
closer, in fact, than their boyfriends
Kylar, Vinnie, John.

Before school
we congregate in small circles
near the school's doors,
the day and its drama
project suspended.

Memory is fickle
yet I remember everything
about her,
trust her
because she is so blonde.

I ask for gum
and she offers me
the wad from her mouth.

I believe her

as when your whole life
depends upon the way
the group makes eye contact.
This isn't a stunt, somehow.
I chew the gum all day
even when it has
become stone.

I revel in almost
swallowing the girl.
I reflect on my gum/stone girlfriend,
save the stone in my bathroom
in tissue
for a year.

Robbie Lawrence
of recent and inexplicable
middle school popularity
advises me to do nice things
for popular people: open doors.
He doesn't ask me why
I ask him for tips.

In October, I don't eat
so that in November
the poet's quinoa and kale
winds up in my mouth.
I believe her because
she is so blonde.

The other writers and I
have congregated in a tight circle.

Gum-palm-mouth.
Poet-to-go box-mouth.

I don't have to explain
the building complicatedness of this
do I?

Map of chewing,
how ingestion and digestion
puzzle,
why some things slide down
and others won't,
how the brain makes euphoria,
how this is a way of
being fed.

2004 Space Odyssey

If the film is famous
for slim dialogue,
I blab enough for
the both of us,
and don't touch
my taco
salad in a bread bowl.

Much later
when recounting this date
to my then girlfriend and her
best friend,
I'm told the
meal sounds like an
abomination
and I don't know if they mean
the taco salad in a bread bowl
or Nancy and I on a date.

Losers have lives too,
and I thought Nancy was a loser
but in reality I was a loser
and Nancy was a
cosmonaut in fishnets.

Her religion
had symbols
like *NIN* and a star
in a circle
and I didn't ask what those meant
and I still don't know
and therein lies the problem with me.
Out at Perkins with her
is a kind of space travel.

It's my first date.
When I don't eat
she calls me out
and I wish my heart unpumped blood.
I want to be girlfriends
so bad and I know
we're doomed.

If somebody asked me
to recreate this scene,
I'd do it,
just give me a Perkins.

I learn her mom
is a chemist.
She has a soft voice
and a tiny mouth.
I realize that in six years
of school together
I've never seen her smile.

The space between
our wicked lies
plays on Perkins' radio
and I'm overcome by a
trembling. Lettuce like ticker tape
and pebbled beef dangles
from the fork which
I can't bring to my mouth.

At the end of the night
we hug at the double doors,
try to hide my sweaty pits,
and I plot to lose the number
she's saved in my Tracfone
before school on Monday.

The Huddle

I guess a perk of moving back
to my grandmother's
hometown is the
ability to visit her old haunts.

Time travel is possible
if you're corporeal.

We drink a pop called
Green River which now
seems toxic.
The flavor is indescribable
        otherworldly
despite being developed in a lab in
Northern Kentucky.

Everything is terrestrial:
the shape of the middle school and the
gum from Stacey Lee's mouth,
the velvety letters of my last
name on the back of that
mustard yellow gym shirt.

I'm new and the buildings are new
but some things are ancient.

Prophecy

first for Kent Johnson / and later for Kass Fleisher

One of our poets is leaving us
you text late in the afternoon,
though not those exact words,
our phone logs still
a secret best kept
between us.

I know what you mean
brace for who
(must be big)
     our   *us*
someone in common,
someone of that time.

Everything about
                    us
even now
is of that time.

You can send a poem.
Could be a week,
a month.

Earlier, in Chicago
at the writer's conference
I didn't know what poetry was,
but M was by my side
up from the bayou.

At the top of a building,
my city and my father's,

a lawyer reads her own copyright page.

Poets all around,
boot heels on hardwoods,
magazines I don't know,
Kent's homage to the last avant garde,
and this, after your death,
      so unwillingly mine.

ACKNOWLEDGMENTS

My great thanks to the following publications for featuring past and present versions of poems in this collection.

Action, Spectacle: "Ekphrasis for plasma"; "Prophecy"

Belt Magazine: "What Story Can We Tell Better"; "At the Water Tower"

The Waggle: "Basket's Lament"

Sheepshead Review: "Leftovers"

South Carolina Review: "Let's Contribute to a Community Free of Sexual Misconduct"

ADVANCE: "Burn tout"; "Runaway Jury"

Sepia: "Great Expectations"

Earlier versions of some poems also appeared in chapbooks published by Finishing Line Press, Press 254/Illinois State University Publications Unit, and Baltic Writing Residency/ Action, Spectacle. My thanks to the editors of those publications for supporting my work.

The epigraph appears in Neko Case's perfect song "At Last." Take a listen.

Finally, a big Midwestern thanks to Cornerstone Press and Dr. Ross K. Tangedal for choosing this book for the Portage Poetry Series, a dynamic series of poetry collections produced by talented students at the University of Wisconsin–Stevens Point, and Sarah Etlinger, a fellow Cornerstone poet who first encouraged me to submit my manuscript. Thank you especially to Paige Biever and Reilly Crous, who provided feedback on this manuscript with generosity and inventiveness. Teaching presses are a treasure, and we must do all we can to ensure their survival in an increasingly consolidated publishing landscape.

Jenna Goldsmith is a poet and writer living in Northern Illinois. She is Senior Instructor I at Oregon State University Cascades and director of the low-residency MFA program in Writing. Her 2022 chapbook *CRUSH* was the winner of the Baltic Writing Residency Chapbook Contest. She was City Poet Laureate of Rockford, Illinois from 2023–2025.

www.ingramcontent.com/pod-product-compliance
Lightning Source LLC
Chambersburg PA
CBHW030510130626
46549CB00007B/2930